Six
VERY EASY
PIECES
IN THE FIRST POSITION
Op. 22.

EDWARD ELGAR

also available for:
Viola with Piano Accompaniment
String Orchestra
Full Orchestra

and also by Edward Elgar:
Études Caracteristiques Op. 24.
(to 7th Position)
for Violin solo

EXCLUSIVELY DISTRIBUTED BY

Hal•Leonard®

Exercices très faciles.

(à la Première position.)

A.

Edward Elgar, Op.22.

710

"Edition Chanot."

Printed and bound in Great Britain by
Caligraving Limited Thetford Norfolk

3/06(58277)

B.
Allegretto.

4

C.
Andante.

D.
Andantino.

E.

Allegretto.

F.
Allegro.

"Edition Chanot."

Printed and bound in Great Britain by
Caligraving Limited Thetford Norfolk
3/06(58277)

Six Very Easy Pieces

Exercices très faciles.

(à la Première position.)

SOLO VIOLIN.
(or 1st Violin in String (or Full) Orchestra)

Edward Elgar, Op. 22.

Bosworth & Co. Ltd.

710